STORIES OF REDEMPTION

STORIES OF REDEMPTION

A DEVOTIONAL JOURNEY THROUGH THE BOOK OF RUTH

TRIP KIMBALL

WORD STRONG
WITH TRIP KIMBALL

❦ Created with Vellum

ENDORSEMENTS

What a really easy to read but insightful glimpse into the story of Ruth and her journey of pain, heartache, redemption, and new life. Trip Kimball captures our hearts as we read of our Kinsmen-Redeemer and the restoration in store for each of us in Jesus Christ.

Pastor Bruce A. Sonnenberg
He Intends Victory

———

Drawing from his experience as a pastor, missionary, ministry leader and life-long student of the Word, Trip Kimball has given us a solid resource for encountering the Book of Ruth and mining the treasures within.

I appreciate how Trip weaves inductive Bible study principles into the book, along with his insights and applications. Highly useful for individual and group study.

Pastor John Cowan
Poimen Ministries | Calvary Chapel Bishop

———

Ruth is one of those hidden gems in the Scriptures that speaks to so many different, deep areas of our lives. From grief and mourning, to bitterness, to hope, to redemption and beyond, God speaks life into any soul who dives into a study of this amazing book of the Bible.

It takes a careful pastoral heart to lead us into the truths of the book of Ruth. You'll be blessed as Pastor Trip takes you through Ruth devotionally. It is not to be read through quickly, but as Trip shows us, it's to be savored, slowly, meditatively, and methodically. Enjoy the time you invest in studying Ruth. You'll be blessed!

Pastor Ed Taylor
Calvary Church, Aurora CO

———

Mining his years of experience as a pastor, missionary, bible college teacher, and discipler, Trip Kimball makes the book of Ruth both alive and relevant for every follower of Jesus in our own day and age.

His ability to describe the historical and cultural context in which Stories of Redemption takes place, and then contextualize the truths about God's gracious willingness and capacity to redeem the stories of our lives today is both refreshing and encouraging.

Pastor Jeff Jackson
Director of Church Relations and Missionary Care
Shepherd's Staff Mission Facilitators

CONTENTS

FOREWORD

Ruth is on a journey. She did not realize as a little girl growing up in the far off country of Moab, on the eastern side of the Dead Sea, that someday you and I would be reading her story, a journey not just from one country to another but from one "set of gods" to the One True Living God!

As her story of loving-kindness and care becomes ours, we are treated to a true love story; a love for family, a love for God, and a love for His wonderful ways.

Trip Kimball has captured the transitioning heart of Ruth as she moves with her mother-in-law, Naomi, back to the land of Promise. Since I have known Trip (now some 54+ years), his tenderness and kindness look much like that of Ruth's.

Watching him grow into spiritual manhood, observing how he and Susan and their kids moved by faith from their home by the sea to a desert place then on to a faraway country, you too will be blessed by Trip's commitment to always reflect God's heart in this story.

This devotional will capture your attention and invite you along this journey as well. You will see, like Ruth, that it is the One True Living

God, Yahweh, who guides us through the most challenging circum-stances of life, only for us to find out that it is His will, all along, that helps us to walk in that same loving-kindness and care.

Bruce A. Sonnenberg

Executive Director/Founder

He Intends Victory

PO Box 53534

Irvine, CA 92619

www.HeIntendsVictory.com

AUTHOR'S NOTE
HERE'S HOW TO GET THE MOST FROM THIS DEVOTIONAL STUDY

The background information and insights in this introduction are helpful for keeping the original context of the Book of Ruth in view.

The devotional studies are intended to be simple and applicable in a personal way. But all application needs to be considered on the basis of the story's original time, culture, and historical context.

The NIV text was used because I prefer using the term *kinsman-redeemer*, which is found in the KJV and NIV 84 versions of the Bible, and *guardian-redeemer* is similar. The NIV is a more readable text for most of us than the traditional KJV. I've also used God's Word Translation (GW) because of the reframing and simplicity of thought it brings.

The text for the larger context of each story is found at the end of each chapter. Some simple study questions for each story are listed after the text.

If you want to get the most out of this little book, allow the study questions to bring you back to the Bible text (your own preferred text is fine) and keep a journal or notebook handy to write down your answers and whatever insights the Holy Spirit may give you.

The most valuable study is your own personal study of God's written Word guided by the Holy Spirit. If what I've shared in these Stories of Redemption is helpful, that's an added benefit and a blessing for me.

INTRODUCTION

Introduction and Background

The Book of Ruth is not a random romantic story, but a significant look at the sovereignty of God and His plan of redemption for all people within the world. It also contains interesting character studies of the main people—Naomi, Ruth, and Boaz.

The Mosaic Law and history of Israel give prophetic insight to make the history of the Bible relevant to our own time. Ruth provides a sort of "God's-eye view" into the history of Israel and the world.

Keep a notebook handy to write down important things you learn as you read and study. The study questions are designed to walk you through the story to observe and interpret what you read in the text, and apply truth that is clarified through the study process. Put yourself in the story, use your imagination to identify with the people involved.

A set of study questions follow each devotional. These questions are designed to help you think about what you're reading and studying within the text itself. These study questions follow the complete Bible text for each devotional at the end of each chapter.

The Book of Ruth— a Story of Redemption

The Book of Ruth, as literature, is a narrative—a story. The value and purpose for studying Ruth and other narratives is learning from the examples of people within the story.

We are given insight into God's relationships and interaction with them along with a view of the character of people. We are able to see their values, beliefs struggles, and other responses towards God, various events, other people, situations in their lives, and whatever else may unfold in the story.

This devotional book is subtitled, *Stories of Redemption*. The book of Ruth contains several vignettes of dialog, events, and insights within the larger context of the book. A redemptive insight can be found in each of them.

Biblical redemption is a theme throughout the Bible, revealing God's reconciliatory and redemptive love for humanity. This theme of redemption extends from the fall of man in the third chapter of Genesis, builds to a climax with the death and resurrection of Jesus, the Son of God, and culminates with a new heaven and earth in the book of Revelation.

Four Important Elements in Stories

There are **four important elements** to take note of while studying narratives: *people, places, events and actions, and time.*

Obviously, people play an important role in stories. Not only the people themselves, but their roles in the story, their heritage and origins, their culture, manners, and customs.

Where the story takes place is important. The geographic locations and regions, travel and distances, the environment people are in, and the physical locations whether it's part of the landscape or a house or tent.

What takes place within the story are actions and events that help bring the story to life. This can include conversations among people, story of how a family line was continued. This is important because it is the family line of King David, and more importantly, the family line of the most important Kinsman-Redeemer—Jesus Christ—also born in Bethlehem.

1

A FLAWED AND FAILED ATTEMPT TO ESCAPE

" *In the days when the judges ruled, there was a famine in the land. So a man from Bethlehem in Judah, together with his wife and two sons, went to live for a while in the country of Moab (Ruth 1:1).*

The people of Israel were ruled by judges for about 340 years. Judges were rescuers sent by God. The nation was in a time of moral and spiritual darkness brought on by idolatry, oppression, and slavery.

God sent these judges to deliver the people from their oppressors to restore freedom and stability. But this freedom only lasted for a season. This cycle of oppression and freedom continued for more than 300 years.

Typically, other nations or tribal groups would subdue the people of Israel into servitude and plunder their crops and livestock. This was one way God dealt with Israel's rebellion towards Him, since it created economic hardship and oppression.

When a severe famine came, one family chose to escape the hardship by moving to a neighboring country—Moab (now part of present-day Jordan).

The escape

A father and mother—Elimelek, whose name means *God is my king*, and Naomi—set out from the region of Judah with their two sons —Mahlon (his name means *sick or weakling*) and Kilion (whose name means *pining or finished*)—to establish a home in this foreign land.

But things did not go well for them in Moab. Naomi's husband died, leaving her widowed with two sons. Naomi's sons married Moabite women, but both of her sons died as well.

Now, Naomi, whose name means *pleasant one*, was stuck in a foreign land as a widow, saddled with the responsibility for her son's widows. It was far from a pleasant situation and she was a long way from her homeland.

In Jewish culture, women had little to no status and no resources to support themselves—especially a widow with two dependent women in a country far from her homeland.

After ten years away, things began to change for the better. Naomi heard of the Lord's plentiful provision in her homeland of Judah and decided to return home with her two daughters-in-law.

A problem with trust

At the beginning of the story in the Book of Ruth, we can see the move to Moab as a flawed and failed attempt to escape God's judgment on Israel.

When you find yourself trusting in other things or someone else, including yourself, remember there is One who is ever-faithful and trustworthy. Even when you can't see how it will help—seek the Lord's guidance and wisdom, and trust in His grace and goodness.

SCRIPTURE TEXT
RUTH 1:1-6

In the days when the judges ruled, there was a famine in the
land. So a man from Bethlehem in Judah, together with his
wife and two sons, went to live for a while in the country of
Moab.
The man's name was Elimelek, his wife's name was Naomi, and
the names of his two sons were Mahlon and Kilion. They were
Ephrathites from Bethlehem, Judah. And they went to Moab
and lived there.
Now Elimelek, Naomi's husband, died, and she was left with her
two sons.
They married Moabite women, one named Orpah and the other
Ruth. After they had lived there about ten years,
both Mahlon and Kilion also died, and Naomi was left without
her two sons and her husband.
When Naomi heard in Moab that the LORD *had come to the aid*
of his people by providing food for them, she and her
daughters-in-law prepared to return home from there.
(Ruth 1:1-6 NIV)

The bitter goodbye

In this part of the story, Naomi plans to return to her homeland with her two widowed daughters-in-law, Orpah (her name means *neck or stubbornness*) and Ruth. As they prepare to head to Judah, Naomi realizes how difficult the travel and transition will be for all three of them.

The two Moabite women would be outsiders back in Judah and Naomi expresses her own bitterness about her situation and blames God for it.

> *"No, my daughters. My bitterness is much worse than yours because the Lord has sent me so much trouble." (Ruth 1:13 GW)*

Naomi urges Orpah and Ruth to return to their own people, land, and gods, then speaks a blessing over them.

As she kisses them goodbye, Orpah and Ruth weep out loud and insist on going back with Naomi. But Naomi tries to reason with them. She doesn't have anything to offer, and they'd be better off remaining in their own familiar homeland.

There's an obvious bond between these women, forged by time and shared hardships. Each is without a husband or children. They've grieved together over their shared family losses.

At this point, Naomi shares her heart in an honest and open way.

> *No, my daughters. My bitterness is much worse than yours because the Lord has sent me so much trouble.*

Again, the women are overwhelmed and erupt with loud grieving over the realization that a choice needs to be made. Naomi clarifies herself, her decision, and the inevitable separation.

 Orpah kisses Naomi goodbye, but Ruth clings to her.

This is a redemptive turning point.

The different choices these women make will be seen to be a significant event as the story unfolds. Ruth's choice will have a future impact revealed later in the extended story of Ruth.

Grief, separation, and choice

Imagine the bond between these three women. They were family and they shared common memories and grief. The two Moabite women seemed to have a sense of hope and shelter in Naomi's God.

Saying goodbye and moving far away brings the reality of separation into clear focus. It is often preceded by and followed by grief. It was especially so in those days. Once they separated, they would never see each other again.

Our present freedom to travel from one place to another was unknown even a century ago, except for the very wealthy. Only those looking to start a new life in a new place would risk this kind of separation. Even then, it isn't without its own often immeasurable costs and losses.

Missionaries who set out for distant lands in years gone by knew the grief and finality of goodbyes and separation from loved ones and their homeland. Most knew they would never return because they didn't have the resources or knew they were destined to die while on the mission field.

Even now, cross-cultural missionaries have a lot of goodbyes to say. Some are much harder than others. Every missionary experiences this not just when they leave but while on the field. You need to learn to say goodbye often as people come and go in your life.

When Susan and I left our family and friends, our home culture, and home church to move to the Philippines, we also left our oldest son to finish school. That was the hardest goodbye and the roughest year for us as a family on the field.

It was conversely difficult when we brought our ministry to a close several years ago and said many final goodbyes. Each goodbye came as a direct result of a choice we made.

There are some goodbyes where others leave and we remain. Some separations are not our choice but the result of circumstances beyond our control.

Where's the redemption in all this?

Redemption can come when we make the choice to say goodbye and move on because we see beyond the separation and grief of those goodbyes. Sometimes it's a matter of faith to see beyond the situation. Other times God's grace and comfort help us move forward in faith.

When our family moved to the Philippines, we could look past the difficulty of leaving our son, friends, and life in the U.S. because God gave us a vision for ministry there. When we left to come back to the U.S. to care for our parents, God blessed us with His grace and comforted us as we moved forward to a new and uncertain future.

Naomi only saw her situation from her point of view. She was bitter and blamed God. Orpah realized the logic of Naomi's choice to go back to her homeland and people. So she chose to stay in her homeland with her people and her gods.

But Ruth saw beyond her situation by faith. She trusted in Naomi's God and had hope. As the story continues, we'll see how pivotal a figure Ruth becomes in these stories of redemption, even the redemption story for all humanity.

 Are you able to see beyond yourself and your life situation by faith?

———

REFLECTION

Times of separation and grief are also times of choice. We can choose to hang on to the bitterness or let it go. We can choose to blame or trust God. We can just see loss or look forward by faith beyond the loss.

———

PRAYER FOCUS

When you face a difficult goodbye or separation, ask the Lord for grace to handle it well, comfort to endure it, and faith to see beyond it.

SCRIPTURE TEXT
RUTH 1:7-14

With her two daughters-in-law she left the place where she had
   been living and set out on the road that would take them back
   to the land of Judah.
Then Naomi said to her two daughters-in-law, "Go back, each of
   you, to your mother's home. May the LORD show you
   kindness, as you have shown kindness to your dead
   husbands and to me.
May the LORD grant that each of you will find rest in the home of
   another husband." Then she kissed them goodbye and they
   wept aloud and said to her, "We will go back with you to your
   people."
But Naomi said, "Return home, my daughters. Why would you
   come with me? Am I going to have any more sons, who could
   become your husbands?
Return home, my daughters; I am too old to have another
   husband. Even if I thought there was still hope for me—even
   if I had a husband tonight and then gave birth to sons
   — would you wait until they grew up? Would you remain
   unmarried for them? No, my daughters. It is more bitter for

me than for you, because the LORD's hand has turned against me!"

At this they wept aloud again. Then Orpah kissed her mother-in-law goodbye, but Ruth clung to her.

(Ruth 1:7-14 NIV)

QUESTIONS TO REVIEW AND CONSIDER

1. What major changes take place in the first chapter so far (up to verse 14)?
2. What happens because of these changes and who is involved?
3. How would you describe the discussion between Naomi and her two daughters-in-law?
4. What is Naomi's view of all that happens?
5. What is the outcome for the two women from Moab and how are they different from one another?

3

THE AMAZING CONFESSION OF A WOMAN OF DESTINY

Story 3

> But Ruth replied, "Don't urge me to leave you or to turn back from you. Where you go I will go, and where you stay I will stay. Your people will be my people and your God my God. (Ruth 1:16)

This is one of my favorite segments of the story of Ruth. It is a pivotal scene in the narrative. This dialog between Naomi and Ruth illustrates important and valuable themes in the book of Ruth and of the Bible's larger narrative arc.

Four important ideas and values stand out to me in this verse—*faith, faithfulness, redemption, and discipleship.*

Faith

Ruth demonstrates great faith with her insistence to travel with Naomi to Judah. Unlike her sister Orpah, Ruth is not returning to her homeland, her people, or their gods. She trusts in the Living God of Israel—

We can claim a sense of objectivity but that's all it is—a sense. Only the Lord sees things in the truest objective way because He is eternal. When God reveals His perspective, as in the Scriptures, we still tend to see it through our own biased lens.

This final vignette of this first chapter of Ruth gives us a glimpse of all three perspectives—Naomi's, the viewpoint of other people, and the actual situation.

The arrival

They happened to enter Bethlehem just when the barley harvest began. (Ruth 1:22 GW).

After Ruth's declaration of commitment to stay with Naomi, they traveled from Moab to Bethlehem in Judah—a journey lasting at least two to three days on foot. It was a difficult and risky journey of at least 30 miles.

As they entered Naomi's hometown, many were excited to see her, and the women wondered at Naomi's presence with a young Moabite widow and no husband. *Can this be Naomi?*

Naomi's response is telling. It reveals how she sees her situation and why it happened. Not only is it subjective, it is filled with self-pity, reflecting her broken heart and spirit.

This limited self-focused perspective is somewhat typical for most of us in similar situations.

Naomi's outlook

She answered them, "Don't call me Naomi [Sweet]. Call me Mara [Bitter] because the Almighty has made my life very bitter. I went away full, but the LORD has brought me back empty. Why do you call me Naomi when the LORD has

> *tormented me and the Almighty has done evil to me?" (Ruth
> 1:20-21 GW)*

Let's review each of Naomi's three statements.

> ❝ *Don't call me Naomi...Call me Mara, because the Almighty
> has made my life very bitter.*

Naomi's name can mean both *pleasant or sweet,* and Mara means *bitter.*
It's a play on words to describe both her inner state and her outlook on
life. She holds God responsible for her situation.

> ❝ *I went away full, but the Lord has brought me back empty.*

Do you see how she puts the blame for her situation on the Lord?
Naomi sees her life's misfortunes as God's hand *against* her and uses a
play on words to make her point. Her statement about going out *full*
but coming back *empty* is her perspective now but will change later in
the story.

> ❝ *Why call me Naomi when the Lord has afflicted me; the
> Almighty has brought misfortune upon me?*

It's pretty clear Naomi is playing on the sympathy of others as a victim
of circumstances though it was her husband's and her choice to leave
Judah ten years before. She only returns because things have reversed.

They left because of a famine. She returns because of God's provision
for Israel. Her answer may be posed as a question, but it's rhetorical—
the answer is clear—the Lord is the cause of her problems.

When things go wrong, most if not all of us are quick to find various
reasons it happened and others to blame. Many blame God for all the
problems in the world. Somehow He is responsible for everyone's
choices and all the bad and evil things that happen.

SCRIPTURE TEXT
RUTH 1:19-22

So the two women went on until they came to Bethlehem. When they arrived in Bethlehem, the whole town was stirred because of them, and the women exclaimed, "Can this be Naomi?"
"Don't call me Naomi," she told them. "Call me Mara, because the Almighty has made my life very bitter.
I went away full, but the Lord has brought me back empty. Why call me Naomi? The Lord has afflicted me; the Almighty has brought misfortune upon me."
So Naomi returned from Moab accompanied by Ruth the Moabite, her daughter-in-law, arriving in Bethlehem as the barley harvest was beginning.
(Ruth 1:19-22 NIV)

QUESTIONS TO REVIEW AND CONSIDER

1. What things take place at the end of this chapter?
2. How is the end of the chapter different than the beginning?
3. Do you see any type of resolve or completion within Chapter 1?
4. Could this be an applicable truth for you and your life?
5. Has the Lord spoken to you, personally, about your need to trust in Him?

> " This was Ruth's plan, but God had a much greater plan.

Now it happened that Ruth ended up in the part of the field that belonged to Boaz, who was from Elimelech's family.

Did Ruth just happen to find the field of Boaz or is there more to the story? Ruth chose to go out to glean, and her choice led her to glean in the field of Boaz.

What may seem as happenstance is no accident. God had a great plan that included Ruth with her initiative and choices, but was far beyond anything she could imagine.

A pastoral scene

Ruth goes out to follow the paid harvesters and glean behind them. After their mid-morning break, Boaz, the owner of the field, came out to check on his workers and the harvest. And he notices Ruth.

The manner of Boaz's greeting to his workers and his observance of Ruth's presence begins to reveal the character of Boaz. He greets them all with a blessing and they, likewise, respond to him with a blessing. It illustrates how Boaz regarded and treated those reaping the harvest—with respect and appreciation.

Boaz knows them and they know him, and he realizes there's a new face among them he doesn't know. When Boaz asks the foreman about her, the foreman speaks well of her and identifies her as the young woman who traveled with Naomi from Moab.

The foreman testifies to Ruth's hard work, as well her asking for permission to glean. Everyone seems to be aware of the goodness of Ruth's character and her commitment to Naomi and the God of Israel. This is unusual and significant since she's a foreigner, a Gentile by birth.

This introduction of Ruth to Boaz provides further insight into Ruth's character and some insight into the integrity of Boaz, which will be revealed and later be tested.

We will also see how human free will is woven together with God's sovereign will in the tapestry of God's story of redemption.

 This is how the story happens but it's not by accident, nor by chance, and it isn't fate.

———

REFLECTION

We tend to categorize events in life as either chance or fate. God is sovereign, but He created us with free will. The history of Israel and of humanity confirms and reveals this. It's a paradox, but the one is not mutually exclusive of the other.

———

PRAYER FOCUS

When faced with decisions and opportunities in life, choose to trust in the Lord. Ask Him for wisdom and guidance. Step out in faith. God honors our free will and guides us according to His will.

SCRIPTURE TEXT
RUTH 2:1-7

*Now Naomi had a relative on her husband's side, a man of
standing from the clan of Elimelek, whose name was Boaz.
And Ruth the Moabite said to Naomi, "Let me go to the fields and
pick up the leftover grain behind anyone in whose eyes I find
favor." Naomi said to her, "Go ahead, my daughter."
So she went out, entered a field and began to glean behind the
harvesters. As it turned out, she was working in a field
belonging to Boaz, who was from the clan of Elimelek.
Just then Boaz arrived from Bethlehem and greeted the harvesters,
"The Lord be with you!" "The Lord bless you!" they answered.
Boaz asked the overseer of his harvesters, "Who does that young
woman belong to?"
The overseer replied, "She is the Moabite who came back from
Moab with Naomi.
She said, 'Please let me glean and gather among the sheaves behind
the harvesters.' She came into the field and has remained here
from morning till now, except for a short rest in the shelter."*
(Ruth 2:1-7 NIV)

QUESTIONS TO REVIEW AND CONSIDER

1. What important information do we get about a new person in the story?
2. How is this man described?
3. What request does Ruth make of Naomi and what is Naomi's response?
4. What takes place according to Ruth's request and action?
5. What are we told about the man Boaz?
6. How does Boaz greet his workers and what do they tell him about Ruth?
7. Do you think this is all by chance?
8. If not, who's plan do you think it is, Naomi's or the Lord's?

WHY ARE YOU PAYING ATTENTION TO ME?

Story 6

> *So Boaz said to Ruth, My daughter, listen to me. Don't go and glean in another field and don't go away from here. Stay here with the women who work for me. Watch the field where the men are harvesting, and follow along after the women.*
>
> *I have told the men not to lay a hand on you. And whenever you are thirsty, go and get a drink from the water jars the men have filled."*
>
> *At this, she bowed down with her face to the ground. She asked him, Why have I found such favor in your eyes that you notice me—a foreigner?" (Ruth 2:8-10)*

One of the existential questions of life is—*Does my life have significance?* Another one is, *Does my life matter to anyone but me?* These are reasonable questions, especially since each of us are one person among 7.7 billion people in the world.

Every human life has significance—even those unborn in the womb—because each person is created in the image of God (Genesis 1:27). This makes each of us significant to God. And all of us are significant to our families.

It's easy to see a good sense of well-being in healthy families. But a person's significance is also seen in dysfunctional families or those torn apart by divorce, mental illness, alcoholism or drug addiction, poverty, war, or any other detrimental situation including death.

My wife and I witnessed this while raising our own children, as foster parents of children in crisis, and later as surrogate parents for the children and abused girls we cared for in the Philippines for nearly a quarter of a century.

Every child—every one of us—has significance and worth, yet at some point, we all wonder what our purpose in life is.

> *"Why are you so helpful? Why are you paying attention to me? I'm only a foreigner" (Ruth 2:10 GW).*

God's favor—His unmerited goodness

As the story of Ruth the Moabitess continues to unfold, we see her surprised at God's favor in her life.

Many people find it difficult to grasp the truth of God's grace—His favor and kindness. Two simple reasons come to mind—we don't deserve it and we can't earn or receive it based on good deeds.

God's favor is given by God for His purposes. He doesn't extend His favor based on a person's goodness, but He does grant it to us for our benefit because He loves us. It's God's blessing, His grace, given to someone for His purposes.

 But how is it possible for someone to receive His favor?

The simplest and most direct way to receive God's favor is to trust in Him—to have faith in Him. Here is what we're told in the book of Hebrews:

> *No one can please God without faith. Whoever goes to God must believe that God exists and that he rewards those who seek him.* (Hebrews 11:6 GW)

Faith in God is an implicit trust in God. This is what we see in Ruth and why she receives God's favor and why Boaz shows her favor. It started when she chose to trust in the God of Naomi—the God of Israel—the One, True, and Living God.

We see her confession of faith when she said,

> *"Your people will be my people, and your God will be my God"* (Ruth 1:16c).

We see God's favor shown to Ruth through Boaz. Why? He knows of her faith in God and her faithfulness in character (Ruth 2:11).

Ruth is unaware of why God's favor rests upon her, but she knows she neither deserved nor earned the favor Boaz bestowed upon her. She experiences it when he tells her to stay in his field, to stay with the young women, and to drink the water drawn by his young men (verses 8-9).

In response to Ruth's wonder at the favor Boaz shows her, Boaz tells her three things he has observed about her that reflect her trust in God and how he sees this working through her life (verse 11).

Then Boaz pronounces a blessing on her. His blessing reveals how and why the Lord's favor is upon her.

> *"May the Lord repay you for what you have done. May you be richly rewarded by the Lord, the God of Israel, under whose wings you have come to take refuge"* (Ruth 2:12).

The provisional and protective care Boaz shows to Ruth is unexpected. It's hard for us to fully comprehend this without understanding the culture of their time. Women, especially widows, had little status. Foreign—Gentile or non-Israelite—women had even less respect in Israelite culture.

Even when we receive God's favor, we should not take it for granted. Ruth's reply to Boaz in verse 13 shows us an appropriate and wise attitude we need to have.

"May I continue to find favor in your eyes, my lord," she said.
"You have put me at ease by speaking kindly to your servant—
though I do not have the standing of one of your servants"
(Ruth 2:13).

Ruth's gratitude seems to compel and prompt Boaz to extend his favor even further, as seen in verses 14-16. Boaz includes Ruth with the rest of his harvesters by inviting her to eat the midday meal with them, then gives his young men special instructions about her.

Gleanings from Ruth

We'll look at the rest of the story next in the next chapter, but consider what we've learned about God's favor in this segment.

When we walk by faith with a childlike trust in God, His favor will be upon us and go before us, as He opens doors of opportunity we can't open on our own. Ruth gains a sense of significance and value because of God's grace.

When Ruth realizes the great favor she's received, she doesn't take it for granted. She's grateful for it and acknowledges this. Ruth's gratitude seems to open further blessing and favor by Boaz.

God's favor, His grace, flows like a stream to carry us along as we learn to rely upon Him with the abandon and commitment we see in Ruth as she trusts in the God of Israel.

We can choose to trust in the Lord but we will never earn or gain God's favor because of our choice. God's grace is His gift to those who trust in Him.

 What have you learned about God's favor in your life and for you?

REFLECTION

When you walk by faith with a childlike trust in God, His favor will be upon you and go before you, as He opens doors of opportunity you can't open on your own. When you realize God's favor in your life—acknowledge it, be grateful for it, rest in it and in Him.

PRAYER FOCUS

While in prayer, learn to wait upon God, listen for Him to speak to your heart. Trust Him for His grace to fill you and carry you as you rest in His faithfulness and goodness.

SCRIPTURE TEXT
RUTH 2:8-16

So Boaz said to Ruth, My daughter, listen to me. Don't go and
glean in another field and don't go away from here. Stay here
with the women who work for me.
Watch the field where the men are harvesting, and follow along
after the women. I have told the men not to lay a hand on
you. And whenever you are thirsty, go and get a drink from the
water jars the men have filled."
At this, she bowed down with her face to the ground. She asked
him, Why have I found such favor in your eyes that you notice
me—a foreigner?"
Boaz replied, I've been told all about what you have done for your
mother-in-law since the death of your husband—how you left
your father and mother and your homeland and came to live
with a people you did not know before.
May the Lord repay you for what you have done. May you be
richly rewarded by the Lord, the God of Israel, under whose
wings you have come to take refuge."
"May I continue to find favor in your eyes, my lord," she said. You
have put me at ease by speaking kindly to your servant—
though I do not have the standing of one of your servants."

At mealtime Boaz said to her, "Come over here. Have some bread and dip it in the wine vinegar." When she sat down with the harvesters, he offered her some roasted grain. She ate all she wanted and had some left over.

As she got up to glean, Boaz gave orders to his men, Let her gather among the sheaves and don't reprimand her.

Even pull out some stalks for her from the bundles and leave them for her to pick up, and don't rebuke her."

(Ruth 2:8-16 NIV)

QUESTIONS TO REVIEW AND CONSIDER

1. How does the conversation between Boaz and Ruth begin?
2. What does Boaz tell Ruth and what is her response to him here?
3. What other things do Boaz and Ruth say to one another?
4. How does Boaz treat Ruth?
5. Was this expected, or do you think this is somewhat unusual for that time?
6. What else does Boaz say to his workers (young men) about Ruth?
7. Do you think he extends special favor to her or is this typical and expected?
8. What does this tell you about Boaz as a man?

A REVERSAL OF FORTUNE OR GOD'S PROVIDENCE?

Story 7

> Her mother-in-law asked her, "Where did you glean today? Where did you work? Blessed be the man who took notice of you!"
>
> Then Ruth told her mother-in-law about the one at whose place she had been working. "The name of the man I worked with today is Boaz," she said.
>
> "The Lord bless him!" Naomi said to her daughter-in-law. "He has not stopped showing his kindness to the living and the dead." She added, "That man is our close relative; he is one of our guardian-redeemers." (Ruth 2:19-20)

When we lose hope—the darkness and isolation seem overwhelming. When faced with failure, it can bring a sense of hopelessness. But when hope returns and blessing is in our grasp, the foreboding sense of hopelessness becomes a distant memory.

This segment of the story of Ruth brings a reversal of attitude on the part of Naomi. She sees it as a reversal of fortune at God's hand. But it's far more than that for two reasons.

God's providence

First off, fortune or luck and God's providence are not the same. Naomi and her family left their home to escape a great famine but things didn't go well. She returns to her homeland "empty" but blames God for her troubles (Ruth 1:21), even though she returned at a time of harvest and provision in Bethlehem (*house of bread*).

Now Bethlehem becomes a place of provision for Naomi and Ruth. Naomi is now able to see how God's hand is upon her. She sees how Ruth's labor in Boaz' fields provide more than food. Naomi has a new hope because of who Boaz is.

God's providence is simply God's provision with His guidance and care. It is neither destiny, nor fate, nor luck. Just as a shepherd leads his sheep, God has led Naomi back to Bethlehem.

Here, we see a prophetic glimpse of God's redemption through His Son Jesus whose birthplace was Bethlehem. Not only was Jesus known as the Good Shepherd, He also referred to Himself as the Bread of Life

> **Jesus said, I am the "Bread of Life" (John 6:35).**

A second reason for Naomi's change of heart is her realization of who owns the field Ruth gleans in and how much favor is shown to her.

On her return from Moab to Bethlehem, Naomi tells her friends the Lord afflicted her and brought her misfortune. In other words, her *bad luck* was God's fault.

But now she says,

> *"He [The Lord] has not stopped showing his kindness to the living and the dead."*

Notice she says—*to the living and the dead.* This is in reference to her husband and two sons who passed away and her faith in a resurrection and eternal life.

Gleanings from Ruth's gleaning

What prompts Naomi's newfound hope in the Lord? A quick review of this segment of the story will help us see why.

At the end of the day—a long day from sunup to sundown—Ruth threshes the barley she gleaned and brings it home to Naomi, along with her leftovers from lunch. When she shows it all to Naomi, her mother-in-law realizes someone has shown her great favor.

When asked where she gleaned, Ruth tells Naomi the man she worked with was named Boaz. Ruth is unaware of who this man is but not Naomi!

> *"That man is our close relative; he is one of our kinsman-redeemers"* (Ruth 2:20 NIV 84).

Ruth has no understanding of why this is significant, but for Naomi, it renews her faith in God and her hope for the future.

The idea of a kinsman-redeemer is foreign to Ruth and perhaps for many of us. It's a provision in the Law of Moses to protect a family's legacy and their property. We'll look at this more closely in chapter 12 (chapter 3 of Ruth). If you want a reference point of understanding, read Leviticus 25:25.

Naomi affirms Boaz's encouragement and the invitation for Ruth to continue working with his young women harvesters. Not just for Ruth's safety and the provision of food, but for the potential of a much greater blessing. This greater blessing will be revealed in the final two chapters.

So, Ruth continues to glean in Boaz's field with the other young women through the barley and wheat harvests. This would include at least two months of time, approximately our April and May, possibly into early June.

Review of redemptive points

The end of chapter two is an important milestone in the story of Ruth. Consider how things have turned around for Naomi from the beginning of the story.

- Naomi leaves her home because of famine but returns after ten years as the barley harvest is beginning (chapter 1).
- Naomi goes out "full" and comes back "empty" (in her words) until Ruth begins to glean in the field of her kinsman-redeemer, Boaz, which renews her hope for the future and seems to restore her trust in God.
- Naomi loses her husband and two sons but gains a loyal and industrious daughter-in-law who becomes a catalyst for much greater provision to come.

There are several redemptive points in the first two chapters of Ruth, but more are revealed in the final two chapters. The author of Ruth uses a telescoping timeframe to help us focus on the most important point of redemption in the book.

Chapter 1 covers about ten years from the family going out from Bethlehem to Naomi's return with Ruth the Moabitess. Chapter 2 covers one harvest time—a period of about two or three months towards the beginning of Israel's calendar year.

Until we look at the next episode in the redemptive stories of Ruth, let me ask you a question—

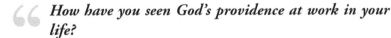 *How have you seen God's providence at work in your life?*

———

REFLECTION

God's providence is simply God's provision with His guidance and care. It is neither destiny nor fate nor is it luck. The Lord—as a shepherd—leads and provides for those who trust in Him, especially those who genuinely rely on Him as a first option.

———

PRAYER FOCUS

As you begin each day, lay it before the Lord—whatever you might have planned or are concerned about. Ask God for His guidance throughout the day. Ask Him for discernment and wisdom and trust Him for His provision. And thank Him through it all!

SCRIPTURE TEXT
RUTH 2:17-23

So Ruth gleaned in the field until evening. Then she threshed the barley she had gathered, and it amounted to about an ephah. She carried it back to town, and her mother-in-law saw how much she had gathered. Ruth also brought out and gave her what she had left over after she had eaten enough.

Her mother-in-law asked her, "Where did you glean today? Where did you work? Blessed be the man who took notice of you!"

Then Ruth told her mother-in-law about the one at whose place she had been working. "The name of the man I worked with today is Boaz," she said.

"The LORD bless him!" Naomi said to her daughter-in-law. "He has not stopped showing his kindness to the living and the dead." She added, "That man is our close relative; he is one of our guardian-redeemers."

Then Ruth the Moabite said, "He even said to me, 'Stay with my workers until they finish harvesting all my grain.'"

Naomi said to Ruth her daughter-in-law, "It will be good for you, my daughter, to go with the women who work for him, because in someone else's field you might be harmed."

So Ruth stayed close to the women of Boaz to glean until the barley and wheat harvests were finished. And she lived with her mother-in-law.

(Ruth 2:17-23 NIV)

QUESTIONS TO REVIEW AND CONSIDER

1. At the end of the day, how much has Ruth gleaned and gathered?
2. What is Naomi's response to Ruth when she returns?
3. How does Naomi respond to Ruth upon learning whose field she worked in?
4. How is what Naomi says here different from what she says to the women who greet them as they enter Bethlehem?
5. What has changed? Why is this important to the story?
6. What is Naomi's further advice to Ruth and how does she respond to Naomi's advice?
7. How long does she stay with the young women harvesters of Boaz?
8. Do you see anything in this chapter relevant for your own life?

8

WHEN WE TRY TO HELP GOD

> *One day Ruth's mother-in-law Naomi said to her, "My daughter, I must find a home for you, where you will be well provided for." (Ruth 3:1)*

"God loves you and people have a wonderful plan for your life!" This is what a good friend of mine would say when people would make suggestions to him or other people. It was a rephrasing of one of the Four Spiritual Laws by the late Bill Bright of Cru (Campus Crusade for Christ)—"God loves you and has a wonderful plan for your life.[1]"

Unfortunately, my friend's rephrasing has a ring of truth to it. My friend and I, along with countless other pastors, have heard well-intentioned suggestions from people in the church many, many times. It goes something like this,

> "Pastor, I think you should..." or "Pastor, the Lord told me to tell you..."

You get the idea.

It is human nature to do this. We all have thoughts about what others should or should not do, or how we might do something better or differently. Even if we don't verbalize these thoughts out loud to others, we still have them.

This could be the byproduct of our self-centered nature. Or, it is our attempt at helping God or even acting like Him in other people's lives. It's something we inherited from our ancestors Adam and Eve after they ate from the tree of the knowledge of good and evil (Genesis 2:17; 3:1-11).

Our plans or God's way?

In chapter three of Ruth, the story takes an important turn. It zeroes in on one relationship within one day.

Although God has His plan and His way for bringing Boaz and Ruth together, Naomi sees the need to step in to help. She spots a way to secure a better future for herself and her daughter-in-law.

> *Naomi, Ruth's mother-in-law, said to her, "My daughter, shouldn't I try to look for a home that would be good for you?" (Ruth 3:1 GW).*

When we view this situation from Naomi's point of view, as best we can, we get an idea of why she sets this plan in motion for Ruth to encounter Boaz in a closer way.

Here's a glimpse into what probably motivated Naomi:

- Bethlehem is Naomi's home town, not Ruth's
- Naomi feels responsible for Ruth the Moabitess whom she brought to Bethlehem
- Naomi understands the customs and traditions of her people in a way Ruth does not

- Naomi sees an opportunity to help Boaz and Ruth come together in marriage
- Naomi understands the role of a kinsman-redeemer (Leviticus 25:25) and how it benefits her
- Naomi knows Ruth will submit to her and whatever advances Boaz makes toward Ruth

This is putting the best construction on things as far as Naomi's motives. But the reality is this—Naomi is trying to manipulate a situation and the people involved (Ruth and Boaz) for her own purposes.

Naomi sees an opportunity and sets her plan in motion. Naomi explains the timing of her plan and describes how Ruth should make herself available to Boaz. Naomi also instructs Ruth how to look and smell her best for the occasion. Naomi adds her final advice to let Boaz take the lead when the time comes.

 This is manipulation, nothing less.

When we try to do similar things in the lives of others, we're being manipulative. In a sense, we see ourselves—like Naomi—helping God in some way. But when we do such things, we often interfere with God and His ways.

Some things to consider

Manipulation takes place in many instances in life. Sometimes it's easier to see how others try to or succeed in manipulating us. This can take place at home within our families or at work with people we know well or not at all.

What is more difficult to see is *our own efforts at manipulating others*, especially when it seems to be necessary from our viewpoint. It's often hard to discern our own motives.

Was Naomi just trying to help move things along with the relationship between Boaz and Ruth? Yes!

Do you think Naomi expected Boaz to take advantage of Ruth in this situation to force something to happen between the two of them? I'll let you decide, but it should be obvious.

What isn't obvious, or perhaps expected, is how both Ruth and Boaz handled themselves in this manipulated situation. We'll see this in the next episode of our stories of redemption in the Book of Ruth.

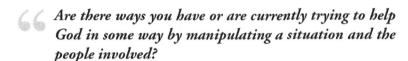

Are there ways you have or are currently trying to help God in some way by manipulating a situation and the people involved?

———

REFLECTION

When we try to do similar things in the lives of others as we see Naomi do, we're being manipulative. When we do such things, we interfere with God and His ways. As has been said before, we don't need to be the Holy Spirit in other people's lives.

———

PRAYER FOCUS

When you find yourself trying to suggest how others ought to be or what they ought to do, stop and repent. Ask the Lord to help you see how you might be doing this with others, and ask Him for the grace to let go and for His forgiveness.

SCRIPTURE TEXT
RUTH 3:1-5

One day Ruth's mother-in-law Naomi said to her, "My daughter, I must find a home for you, where you will be well provided for.
Now Boaz, with whose women you have worked, is a relative of ours. Tonight he will be winnowing barley on the threshing floor. Wash, put on perfume, and get dressed in your best clothes.
Then go down to the threshing floor, but don't let him know you are there until he has finished eating and drinking. When he lies down, note the place where he is lying. Then go and uncover his feet and lie down. He will tell you what to do."
"I will do whatever you say," Ruth answered.
(Ruth 3:1-5 NIV)

QUESTIONS TO REVIEW AND CONSIDER

1. What does Naomi want to do for Ruth and what does she tell Ruth to do?
2. What does it sound like Naomi is trying to do?
3. Do you think this is a good thing, a manipulative plan, or the Lord's direction?
4. What is Ruth's response to Naomi?
5. Have you either been manipulated by others or been a manipulator?

9

WHEN GOD INTERRUPTS OUR PLANS

Story 9

> *When Boaz had finished eating and drinking and was in good spirits, he went over to lie down at the far end of the grain pile. Ruth approached quietly, uncovered his feet and lay down.*
>
> *In the middle of the night something startled the man; he turned—and there was a woman lying at his feet! "Who are you?" he asked. "I am your servant Ruth," she said. "Spread the corner of your garment over me, since you are a guardian-redeemer of our family." (Ruth 3:7-9)*

It's good to have a sense of purpose. It's also helpful to have the vision to see how to pursue and fulfill that purpose. But along the way, circumstances we don't know of may hinder us or seem as obstacles to overcome.

This is true for all of our lives. We make plans based on what we know. However, we don't know everything. But God does. He is omniscient, all-knowing. God knows all there is to know—past, present, and future—because He is eternal in nature.

What is amazing to me is how the Lord works in concert with us. He neither ignores nor rejects our free will but includes it as He orchestrates how His will is worked out.

This next segment in the story of Ruth gives some insight into how God incorporates and works with our free will and plans in conjunction with His will.

When different plans converge

> *"Spread the corner of your garment over me because you are a close relative who can take care of me" (Ruth 3:9 GW).*

As this chapter begins, Naomi lays out her plan for Ruth to follow. Ruth does what she's told, but also has her own idea of how things should go. Our third person in this story, Boaz, reveals new information Naomi and Ruth are unaware of, and sets in motion his own plan.

Each of these three main characters has their own view of what they see happening in the future. Yet God has an overarching plan that reaches beyond their lives.

There's more to this short story segment than grand plans. The encounter on the threshing floor between Boaz and Ruth further reveals insights into each of their characters.

This scene unfolds late in the evening after Boaz finishes the work of separating the grain from the husks. It was backbreaking but rewarding work to prepare the final product of the harvest for sale to others.

Once the work is done for the day, Boaz eats his evening meal and drinks to a point of contentment to rest for the night. He is tired in a good way, which helps him ignore the dust, the hard floor, and his need for a bath, so he lays at the foot of his day's work against the pile of grain.

Ruth watches for her cue to set Naomi's plan in action. Once Boaz is asleep, Ruth quietly tiptoes to where he is sleeping and uncovers his feet and lays down in the darkness.

Later in the night, Boaz wakens because of a chill and realizes someone is lying at his feet. Startled, he asks who it is. Then Ruth sets her plan in motion. She offers herself to Boaz and requests him to cover her with his garment.

Ruth shows her submission to Boaz as a husband-to-be. This is a commitment of trust and love for Boaz.

> 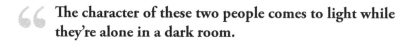 **The character of these two people comes to light while they're alone in a dark room.**

Ruth submitted herself first to Naomi in going to the threshing floor when she does. Now she submits herself to Boaz with the innocence and trust of a child.

Instead of taking advantage of this young foreign woman, Boaz upholds her integrity of character, as expressed in verse 11,

> *"All my fellow townsmen know that you are a woman of noble character."*

A nearer kinsman-redeemer

Boaz also expresses his willingness to be the kinsman-redeemer for Ruth and Naomi but shares some new information that interrupts all their plans. There is another relative more closely related to Elimelech's family line than Boaz.

> It is true that I am a close relative of yours, but there is a relative closer than I. (Ruth 3:12 GW)

This puts Naomi and Ruth's plans on hold but not for long. Boaz vows to resolve the situation the next morning and assures Ruth of his commitment and willingness to take her as his wife and preserve the legacy of the property and lineage of Elimelech and his sons, if possible.

We'll look at the provision in the Mosaic Law to preserve a family's legacy of property later in chapter 13, and why the other relative presents a dilemma to resolve, as the story continues in chapter 4 of the Book of Ruth.

But for now, let's dig a little deeper in this segment of the story found in Ruth chapter 3.

Consider what this short story reveals

Naomi's plan was to set Ruth in a situation she hoped would develop into a marriage relationship to preserve her husband's and son's legacy and their family share of the property.

Ruth looked to Boaz as a provider and protector, not just for herself but also for Naomi. Her request of Boaz reveals this when she says, "Spread the corner of your garment over me, since you are a kinsman-redeemer" (Ruth 3:9 NIV 84).

It is more than an attitude of submission. It is an expression of trust. It reaches back to her commitment to Naomi and trust in the God of Israel. It looks forward to a hoped-for union with Boaz as her kins-man-redeemer, which foreshadows the Kinsman-Redeemer of all.

Although Ruth would have no concept or understanding of a future redeemer, what she says to Boaz echoes the confidence Job had in God when he said, "I know that my Redeemer lives, and that in the end he will stand upon the earth." (Job 19:25 NIV 84)

We all have plans within any given day, whether small or great, routine or extraordinary. But life tends to interrupt our plans, and reality breaks into our daydreams and ideal intentions.

We can allow these interruptions to throw us into fretting, worrying, anger, and resentment, or peace and trust. It depends on what or where or who we put our trust—that is, the focus of our faith.

So, the question is—

 How do you handle the interruptions of life?

———

REFLECTION

We can allow the interruptions that come into our lives to throw us into fretting, worrying, anger, and resentment, or peace and trust. It all depends on what or where or who we put our trust in.

———

PRAYER FOCUS

When you find your life interrupted, choose to lift the eyes of your heart and the thoughts of your mind to the Lord. Not to question but to listen and trust. Learn to trust in God as a first resort rather than out of desperation or frustration.

SCRIPTURE TEXT

RUTH 3:6-13

So she went down to the threshing floor and did everything her mother-in-law told her to do.

When Boaz had finished eating and drinking and was in good spirits, he went over to lie down at the far end of the grain pile. Ruth approached quietly, uncovered his feet and lay down.

In the middle of the night something startled the man; he turned —and there was a woman lying at his feet! "Who are you?" he asked. "I am your servant Ruth," she said. "Spread the corner of your garment over me, since you are a guardian-redeemer of our family."

"The L<small>ORD</small> bless you, my daughter," he replied. "This kindness is greater than that which you showed earlier: You have not run after the younger men, whether rich or poor. And now, my daughter, don't be afraid. I will do for you all you ask. All the people of my town know that you are a woman of noble character.

Although it is true that I am a guardian-redeemer of our family, there is another who is more closely related than I. Stay here for the night, and in the morning if he wants to do his duty as your guardian-redeemer, good; let him redeem you. But if he is not willing, as surely as the LORD lives I will do it. Lie here until morning."

(Ruth 3:6-13 NIV)

QUESTIONS TO REVIEW AND CONSIDER

1. What does Ruth actually do and when does she go to the threshing floor?
2. Does this seem right to you or was this culturally appropriate for those days?
3. What is Boaz's response when he discovers Ruth?
4. What happens next and what request does Ruth make of Boaz?
5. Is this culturally proper? Is this what Naomi told her to do?
6. What actually takes place between Boaz and Ruth (as told in the text)?
7. What does this tell you about their character and how does Boaz confirm this?
8. What important commitment does Boaz make to Ruth?
9. What is the actual situation regarding his relationship to Ruth's family and why is this important?

10

WAITING FOR AN OUTCOME

Story 10

66 *Then Naomi said, "Wait, my daughter, until you find out what happens. For the man will not rest until the matter is settled today." (Ruth 3:18)*

W aiting is something most of us don't do well. Come to think of it, I don't know anyone who does it well in a consistent manner. We might like suspense in a story, but not so much in real life.

American culture is focused on *not* waiting. We want things now not next week, next month, or next year. Conjecture about what could, might, or should happen fills online and mainstream media. This applies to politics, world events, sports, and the lives of celebrities.

When we send a text or email and don't receive a timely reply—like, *immediately*—we're either offended or wonder what's wrong! Go to most stores and you'll find more ready-to-eat or quick-to-prepare food available than the ingredients needed for making a meal from scratch.

Is the drive-through line too slow? Orders are taken before you get to the speaker and menu at some fast-food places. If that's still too slow, *there's an App for that!* to get your order in and done so you don't have to wait at all!

 Who wants to wait? No one!

The word *wait* or similar phrases about waiting occur throughout the Bible. Either as an exhortation or an observation of what people did. It may not be what we want to do, but is often what we need to do.

> *"Stay here, my daughter, until you know how it turns out. The man won't rest unless he settles this matter today" (Ruth 3:18 GW).*

Waiting to find out what will happen

This last segment of chapter three may not seem so important but it holds a valuable truth applicable to all.

After Boaz discovers Ruth lying at his feet in the dark on the threshing floor, he tells her to wait until morning. He makes a commitment to resolve whether or not he can fulfill her request of taking her as his wife.

In the morning, before she leaves to return home to Naomi, Boaz sends Ruth back with six measures of barley. This is a wise move on his part.

Although we don't know the exact amount, these six measures could have weighed as much as sixty pounds, which is why Boaz tells Ruth, "Stretch out the cape you're wearing and hold it tight."

 Why would Boaz do this?

Boaz knew Naomi set this situation up. He knew Ruth the Moabitess would not know or understand about the kinsman-redeemer provision in the Mosaic Law (Leviticus 25:25). Boaz wanted to reassure Naomi of the commitment he made to Ruth.

When Ruth returns home to Naomi, she shares what happened at the threshing floor, what Boaz said, and shows her a large amount of barley grain. Boaz sent a message to Naomi with this grain, a show of good faith on his promise to Ruth.

Naomi accepts this pledge from Boaz and advises her daughter-in-law to wait. She also assures Ruth of a quick resolution to the question of whether Boaz or the other relative would be Ruth's husband and the kinsman-redeemer of the family property.

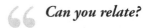 *Can you relate?*

Obviously, Ruth wants to have Boaz for her husband. She knows him, respects him, and trusts him. There's a course of action that needs to take place. It can't be hurried or interrupted.

Ruth and Naomi wait

As the story continues in the book's final chapter, we'll see Ruth doesn't have to wait too long. But it isn't always that way in our lives. Not everything has a simple or timely resolution.

I see many times in my own life where the wait was significant. I remember seeing others move forward in ministry work I also wanted to do. Had I stepped out prematurely, things would not have gone well. I only realized this from waiting.

This also applies to prayer—whether for our own life or when praying for others. Some of my requests and petitions and intercessions in prayer are still not answered. But I know to continue to pray and not give up unless the Lord makes it clear He has answered my prayer. (Luke 18:1).

Sometimes we wait for answers already given but they weren't the answers we wanted or expected. This is where discernment is needed with a genuine trust in God as a Father who always has our best interest in mind.

 Have you learned how to wait with a genuine trust in the Lord?

———

REFLECTION

Wait for the Lord; be strong and take heart and wait for the Lord. (Psalm 27:14 NIV)

Be still before the Lord and wait patiently for him. (Psalm 37:7 NIV)

For God alone, O my soul, wait in silence, for my hope is from him. (Psalm 62.5 ESV)

———

PRAYER FOCUS

When you come to a life situation where you need to wait on God, ask Him for the grace and confidence to trust Him, and thank Him in advance as an expression of trust.

SCRIPTURE TEXT
RUTH 3:14-18

*So she lay at his feet until morning, but got up before anyone could
be recognized; and he said, "No one must know that a woman
came to the threshing floor."*
*He also said, "Bring me the shawl you are wearing and hold it
out." When she did so, he poured into it six measures of barley
and placed the bundle on her. Then he went back to town.*
*When Ruth came to her mother-in-law, Naomi asked, "How did
it go, my daughter?" Then she told her everything Boaz had
done for her*
*and added, "He gave me these six measures of barley, saying, 'Don't
go back to your mother-in-law empty-handed.'"*
*Then Naomi said, "Wait, my daughter, until you find out what
happens. For the man will not rest until the matter is settled
today."*
(Ruth 3:14-18 NIV)

QUESTIONS TO REVIEW AND CONSIDER

1. What takes place that night after Boaz declares his intentions and commitment?
2. What does Boaz do to indicate his intentions to Naomi?
3. What does Ruth tell Naomi when she returns in the morning?
4. What is Naomi's response to Ruth when she hears of what Boaz says, does, and is planning to do?
5. Do you think all of this is because of Naomi's plan or God's?
6. What makes you believe this (either way)?
7. What lesson could you apply in your own life from Chapter 3?

11

JUMPING TO CONCLUSIONS AND TOO QUICK TO COMMIT

Story 11

>   *Then he said to the guardian-redeemer, "Naomi, who has come back from Moab, is selling the piece of land that belonged to our relative Elimelek.*
>
>   *I thought I should bring the matter to your attention and suggest that you buy it in the presence of these seated here and in the presence of the elders of my people.*
>
>   *If you will redeem it, do so. But if you will not, tell me, so I will know. For no one has the right to do it except you, and I am next in line."*
>
>   *"I will redeem it," he said. (Ruth 4:3-4)*

"You'll know a good thing when you see it," is a common saying but it's also true "things are not always as they seem." As far as good things, another common saying is, 'If it seems too good to be true, it probably is."

I often hear people repeat clichés and platitudes like these as if they carry great significance. They don't. When something is spoken over and over again, it begins to lose its original meaning and value.

The same goes for wanting or wishing for something better or more than what we already have. Winning the lottery loses its luster quickly with all the unintended consequences winning brings—high taxes, expectations of family and friends, difficulties of managing wealth, and so on.

I've known pastors of small churches who want bigger ones because they think it would be better. Or, small business owners who want to grow their business bigger for greater income. But bigger is not always better. It brings new challenges and demands many people are not equipped to handle.

I remember observing this as our church body and the other ministries we oversaw grew from start to small to bigger. The changes are dynamic and exponential. These changes impact relationships and the responsibilities and roles required with new growth and expansion.

It can be good, but the responsibilities that come with growth and new opportunities are always challenging.

> *"If you wish to buy back the property, you can buy back the property. But if you do not wish to buy back the property, tell me. Then I will know that I am next in line because there is no other relative except me" (Ruth 4:4 GW).*

Opportunity brings responsibility

As chapter four of Ruth begins, we see Boaz seek out the man who was a closer relative to Elimelech's family than him. Boaz understood the responsibility of being a kinsman-redeemer. It wasn't just about marriage or property.

The role of a kinsman-redeemer was about legacy, the continuation of a family line that could be traced back to the patriarchs of Israel. This legacy was greater than Ruth or Naomi or him. There was a sacred trust to be respected and valued.

Boaz understood the gravity of the situation, so he makes sure there are trustworthy men present to witness what he will share with the other kinsman-redeemer. It was an opportunity that carried a great responsibility.

This scene takes place at the city gate. This would be somewhat similar to the public squares common in older towns and cities. It would be a public hearing that carried legal and binding commitments.

It might seem Boaz is setting up some kind of trap for the nearer relative. But it isn't manipulation in an unethical sense. He set the stage to reveal the true intentions of the other man and himself before the witnesses at the gate.

When presented with the opportunity to acquire property, this man is quick to commit. But there's more responsibility attached to this property than merely purchasing it. There's also more to the story, but we'll look at that in the next chapter.

Consider before you commit

Here's the problem with quick decisions and commitments—there's often more to consider than what we see, hear, or know at first. Most anything of real value requires more attention or responsibility than things of lesser value.

Before making a commitment, we need discernment to assess what we are committing ourselves to with the understanding of the need to be faithful to our commitment once we make it.

 Are there times when you've been too quick to commit to something or someone?

———

REFLECTION

Opportunities always bring certain responsibilities and require a commitment to gain whatever the opportunity holds. Before you commit, ask questions to understand what your responsibilities will be and whether or not you can fulfill it.

Prayer Focus

When faced with challenges or opportunities, be quick to ask God for wisdom and discernment, and the grace needed to make wise commitments.

SCRIPTURE TEXT
RUTH 4:1-4

Meanwhile Boaz went up to the town gate and sat down there just as the guardian-redeemer he had mentioned came along. Boaz said, "Come over here, my friend, and sit down." So he went over and sat down.

Boaz took ten of the elders of the town and said, "Sit here," and they did so.

Then he said to the guardian-redeemer, "Naomi, who has come back from Moab, is selling the piece of land that belonged to our relative Elimelek.

I thought I should bring the matter to your attention and suggest that you buy it in the presence of these seated here and in the presence of the elders of my people.

If you will redeem it, do so. But if you will not, tell me, so I will know. For no one has the right to do it except you, and I am next in line."

"I will redeem it," he said.

(Ruth 4:1-4 NIV)

QUESTIONS TO REVIEW AND CONSIDER

1. What does Boaz do the next day after his commitment to Ruth at the threshing floor?
2. How does Boaz present the situation to this other "guardian-redeemer" (kinsman-redeemer)?
3. Do you think Boaz might be manipulating the situation or would this be the usual way to present it?
4. Why does Boaz need to offer the land to this other man?
5. What does this show you about making commitments?

12

I CANNOT ASSUME THAT RESPONSIBILITY

Story 12

> " *Then Boaz said, "On the day you buy the land from Naomi, you also acquire Ruth the Moabite, the dead man's widow, in order to maintain the name of the dead with his property."*
>
> *At this, the guardian-redeemer said, "Then I cannot redeem it because I might endanger my own estate. You redeem it yourself. I cannot do it." (Ruth 4:5-6)*

Have you ever made a commitment you couldn't keep or made a decision you later regretted? I'm sure we've all done both at some point in our lives. As mentioned in the previous chapter, it's easy to jump to conclusions or make commitments too quickly.

When you or I make a decision or commitment and later go back on our word, it's because we didn't realize the responsibility involved with our decision or commitment.

Some decisions we regret are the ones we *didn't* make but later wished we had. Other commitments are beyond our scope of understanding, and some are rash and impetuous.

I've painted a lot in my life but not as an artist. More than a few times, I bid painting jobs too low because I needed the money right away. I underestimated how long a job would take and overestimated my ability to do it.

Each time, when I realized my mistake, I would try to renegotiate the price. But this was rarely successful. Then I was faced with a further decision—to quit or to finish the job. Finishing it could mean doing a month's worth of work for a week's wages.

We might keep a commitment even though it costs us to do so. But there are times when the wise decision is to suffer loss to our pride and admit we can't fulfill our commitment.

> *"Take all my rights to buy back the property for yourself, because I cannot assume that responsibility" (Ruth 4:6 GW).*

Looking ahead to our redemption

When the nearest kinsman-redeemer realizes buying the property of his relative Elimelech requires marriage to Ruth the Moabite, he reneges on his commitment.

If he married Ruth, he would give up his own legacy of family and property. Marrying Ruth would extend the family lineage of Elimelech but interfere or end his own family line and legacy. It's also probable that the man was already married. So, he deferred to Boaz. And Boaz was willing to accept this responsibility.

At this point in the story, Boaz can become the kinsman-redeemer for Ruth and Elimelech's property and family line. He also becomes a figurative type of Christ—the ultimate Kinsman-Redeemer.

To understand the significance of this situation requires some explanation and looking ahead to the New Testament Scriptures. A figurative type is when a person, event, or thing is a picture of something or someone greater in the future.

A simple example is when Abraham was willing to offer his only son Isaac as a sacrifice (Genesis. 22:1-14). The angel of the Lord intervenes and Abraham figuratively receives his son back from the dead, as it says in the book of Hebrews (Hebrews 11:19).

 This is a prophetic picture of God the Father sending His Son Jesus as an atoning sacrifice for all humanity.

When Jesus died on the cross, He paid or atoned for all humanity's sin. His resurrection from the dead also conquered the power of sin to complete the redemption of all those who trust in Him.

The responsibility of redemption

When the first human, Adam, lived on earth, he was innocent of sin and lived in the paradise of the Garden of Eden. But when the man and his wife selfishly chose to eat what was forbidden to them, they lost their innocence and were sent out of paradise (Genesis 2:7-9; 3:6-11, 15-17, 22-24).

Why did Jesus need to come as a Savior for all humanity? Because none of us are able to free ourselves from the consequence and power of sin. We cannot restore our innocence, that is, our state of not having a sin nature—a selfish nature.

We are like Adam who is represented in a figurative sense by the unnamed kinsman-redeemer in the story of Ruth. This man could not accept the responsibility of redemption. Neither can you or I. It is beyond our ability. We are incapable of overcoming the power and consequence of sin on our own (Romans 3:20-26; 5:18-21).

When Jesus came—as the perfect God-Man—He came to redeem all humanity, for all time, from all sin and its consequence and power. He came to reconcile and restore the close relationship with God lost in the Garden.

Boaz was willing and able to accept the responsibility as a kinsman-redeemer of Ruth and the property and legacy of Elimelech. He set aside his own legacy for the sake of Ruth a Moabite—a gentile—just as Jesus set aside His glory for the sake of all humanity (Philippians 2:5-8).

This Moabite woman—an outsider, a foreigner—was included in the Jewish lineage of Elimelech. This is an important event to consider, but we'll look at it another time.

 Do you understand how each of us is unable to redeem ourselves from the consequence and power of sin?

Take some time to review the thoughts I've shared in this devotional and the related Scripture references.

Consider and reflect on all this and ask the Lord to give you a clearer understanding of the fullness of His redemptive work for all of us on the cross.

———

REFLECTION

None of us are able to redeem ourselves from the power and consequence of sin. This is why Jesus came as the Kinsman-Redeemer of all humanity—for all time and for all sin.

———

PRAYER FOCUS

If you've already trusted in the Lord's redemption, praise Him and give thanks as you go through your day. If you haven't yet, ask the Lord Jesus to give you an understanding of why you need to trust Him for His redemption of your life

SCRIPTURE TEXT

RUTH 4:4-8

I thought I should bring the matter to your attention and suggest that you buy it in the presence of these seated here and in the presence of the elders of my people.

If you will redeem it, do so. But if you will not, tell me, so I will know. For no one has the right to do it except you, and I am next in line." "I will redeem it," he said.

Then Boaz said, "On the day you buy the land from Naomi, you also acquire Ruth the Moabite, the dead man's widow, in order to maintain the name of the dead with his property."

At this, the guardian-redeemer said, "Then I cannot redeem it because I might endanger my own estate. You redeem it yourself. I cannot do it."

(Now in earlier times in Israel, for the redemption and transfer of property to become final, one party took off his sandal and gave it to the other. This was the method of legalizing transactions in Israel.)

So the guardian-redeemer said to Boaz, "Buy it yourself." And he removed his sandal

(Ruth 4:4-8 NIV)

QUESTIONS TO REVIEW AND CONSIDER

1. How does Boaz present the situation to redeem the land of Elimelek's family?
2. Why does the man refuse to accept the purchase of this land, after indicating he wanted it before?
3. How does he show his refusal and why is this done? (You may need to refer to Deuteronomy 25:5-10)
4. What simple life lesson can be drawn from this part of the story for you?

from the word *to redeem*. In Hebrew it is אָל‎–*ga-al* or *go-el* in its transliterated form.

Not only is the family legacy restored, the widow is restored with the status of marriage, no longer alone or dependent on others, and included in the family's legacy.

Consider how this works for Ruth the Moabite, a Gentile (non-Israeli). Though she is a foreigner, she is included as if she were born into the family because of Boaz's commitment to marry her. Unlike her sister-in-law Orpah, Ruth trusted in the God of Israel, which brought great blessing to her life.

 God's redemption brings restoration.

The commitment and role of a kinsman-redeemer are important and significant. Boaz makes sure it is witnessed so it complies with the Law of Moses and the customs of that time.

The witnesses at the city gate included elders from the community—men of influence and status. They acknowledge the commitment of Boaz and pronounce a blessing on Ruth, Boaz, and their offspring. As will be seen in the last segment of the story of Ruth, their blessing reaches beyond the morning of this transaction.

Although it may seem from the words used in the text that Ruth is "bought" with the property, this is not the case. Redemption isn't a mere legal transaction or purchase or repurchase, it is a process of restoration.

 Restoration is always the intent of the Lord in redemption.

Jesus—our great Kinsman-Redeemer

This is why Jesus is the great Kinsman-Redeemer. He repurchased all humanity back from our indebtedness and judgment because of sin.

He did this with His atoning sacrifice on the cross, as explained in the previous devotional chapter.

Why? To restore us into relationship with God and fellowship with the family of God those who trust in God, even as Ruth trusted in the God of Israel.

King David was chosen to be king of Israel because he was a man after God's own heart (1 Samuel 13:14) and is a direct descendant of Boaz, as we see at the end of the Book of Ruth. David was a beloved king and warrior of Israel.

When he fell into moral failure with Bathsheba, David attempted to cover it up by having her husband Uriah murdered. But David's sin was exposed by the prophet Nathan (2 Samuel 12:1-9).

Redemption and restoration are what King David knew after he repented from his sin with Bathsheba and Uriah (Psalm 51:12). David expressed this with assurance in Psalm 23—*He restores my soul (Psalm 23:3).*

Regardless of our mistakes and failures in life, God desires for all of us to personally know His redemption and restoration just as David did.

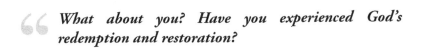

> *What about you? Have you experienced God's redemption and restoration?*

———

REFLECTION

Mercy and grace are the basis for all of God's redemptive work. Restoration is always the intent of the Lord in redemption.

———

PRAYER FOCUS

When you find yourself struggling in your faith, remember to reach out to God in prayer and ask Him to restore you by His mercy and grace.

SCRIPTURE TEXT
RUTH 4:9-12

Then Boaz announced to the elders and all the people, "Today you
are witnesses that I have bought from Naomi all the property
of Elimelek, Kilion and Mahlon.
I have also acquired Ruth the Moabite, Mahlon's widow, as my
wife, in order to maintain the name of the dead with his
property, so that his name will not disappear from among his
family or from his hometown. Today you are witnesses!"
Then the elders and all the people at the gate said, "We are
witnesses.
May the LORD *make the woman who is coming into your home*
like Rachel and Leah, who together built up the family of
Israel.
May you have standing in Ephrathah and be famous in
Bethlehem. Through the offspring the LORD *gives you by this*
young woman, may your family be like that of Perez, whom
Tamar bore to Judah."
(Ruth 4:9-12 NIV)

QUESTIONS TO REVIEW AND CONSIDER

1. What does Boaz do and say when the man will not buy the land?
2. Who does Boaz speak to and how do these men respond to Boaz about this?
3. Who else hears Boaz's commitment and what do they say?
4. What things stand out to you about the people's blessings upon Boaz in verses 11-12?
5. Why do you think the last verse (12) would be significant?
6. What is your understanding and experience with God's redemptive grace and love?

COMING FULL CIRCLE

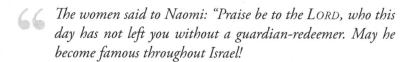

Story 14

> The women said to Naomi: "Praise be to the LORD, who this day has not left you without a guardian-redeemer. May he become famous throughout Israel!
>
> He will renew your life and sustain you in your old age. For your daughter-in-law, who loves you and who is better to you than seven sons, has given him birth."
>
> Then Naomi took the child in her arms and cared for him. The women living there said, "Naomi has a son!" (Ruth 4:14-17)

We tend to think of completion with the phrase *coming full circle*. But a circle has no beginning or end. We can determine a start and end point but those would be arbitrary or theoretical.

A circle is the closest we come to a sense of continuity within our finite world. We can try to imagine eternity and try to grasp the concept of eternity but it is literally beyond us. The symbol we have for infinity is like a sideways figure eight—two circles looped together as a continuous line.

God is eternal in nature. He is the Self-Existent One (Revelation 1:8; 22:13) as He told Moses, *"I AM WHO I AM"* (Exodus 3:14 [*also see John 8:58*]).

God isn't restricted within eternity, for He is the One who created all there is and sustains all there is within eternity. He is both inside and outside eternity at the same time. He is beyond our capacity to fully understand or He wouldn't be God.

> *The women said to Naomi, "Praise the Lord, who has remembered today to give you someone who will take care of you. The child's name will be famous in Israel. He will bring you a new life and support you in your old age. Your daughter-in-law who loves you is better to you than seven sons, because she has given birth" (Ruth 4:14-15 GW).*

Full circle and more

The end of the story of Ruth gives us a glimpse into how coming full circle has a beginning and end only as we view it within history. Yet there's far more in these last few verses than the culmination of the story of a Moabite woman named Ruth.

Before we look at some insights from these last few verses, let's consider all that takes place. Boaz follows through on his commitment to marry Ruth. She becomes pregnant as they consummate their marriage and gives birth to a son.

The women of Bethlehem rejoice with Naomi and bless her with encouraging words of how the Lord as shown His care and love with the birth of her grandson and how great a blessing Ruth is to her.

Naomi becomes a nanny to her grandson named Obed who will become the father of Jesse and grandfather of King David. The story ends with a significant genealogy, which looks ahead a few generations and beyond (see Scripture text at the end).

Why is this genealogy added at the end of Ruth?

God made a great promise to King David to establish his lineage and kingdom forever. This is one of the great promises of the Messiah who would come to redeem Israel (2 Samuel 7:16).

It's a reminder how the story of Ruth the Moabite is significant.

During a dark time in the history of Israel, we see how the lineage of Abraham was preserved through King David to the birth of Jesus. In fact, Ruth is named in the genealogy of Jesus in the Gospel of Matthew (Matthew 1:5).

Some Redemptive insights

At the beginning of Ruth in Chapter 1, the focus is on emptiness with a sense of futility. Naomi expresses it this way "I went away full, but the Lord has brought me back empty" (Ruth 1:21).

She, her husband, and two sons flee the famine in their homeland in hope of a better life. But Naomi loses her husband and two sons with no hope of a family legacy. She's also saddled with the responsibility for two Moabite widows, her daughters-in-law.

When the story is completed, Naomi is full again not empty. In fact, the women of Bethlehem say she is better off than before. The women encourage Naomi about Ruth, *"who loves you and who is better to you than seven sons."*

God sent a kinsman-redeemer to preserve the family legacy of property. Now Naomi has a grandson and is assured of her family caring for her in old age.

 Do you think the Old Testament isn't relevant today? Think again!

This is just one of many stories in the Old Testament highlighting the importance and significance of women. It is somewhat of a redemption for the first woman on earth who ate from the forbidden tree.

The child born to Ruth and Boaz becomes the father of Jesse and grandfather of Israel's most loved king, David. Consider how inclusive and far-reaching this is. This short genealogy of ten generations is repeated almost word for word in Matthew 1:3-6.

This genealogy is part of the line of Judah—the family line of David through whom the Messiah would come, as the ultimate Kinsman-Redeemer. Judah had incestuous relations with his scorned daughter-in-law Tamar, which results in the birth of Perez.

Many generations later, Boaz is born from the union of Salmon and Rahab—the same Rahab who sheltered the two men sent by Joshua to spy out Jericho in the land promised to Abraham. Rahab was a Gentile prostitute and yet she was included in the Messianic family line of Israel!

The three women mentioned in Matthew's account of these same generations—Tamar, Rahab, and Ruth—should not be included in the Messianic line according to Mosaic Law and Jewish tradition but they are. Their inclusion is a reminder of God's inclusive grace, which ought to be a great encouragement to all people.

The full circle

The story of Ruth begins with an interrupted generation (Elimelech and sons) and concludes with a completed generation within ten historically important generations of Israel. What a great reminder how our life stories, at whatever point they are, are not yet complete.

The book of Ruth, with all its stories of redemption, gives us an opportunity to be mindful of God's redemptive grace in our life.

May it help us reflect on how each of our life stories is part of the greater story arc of all humanity and God's redemptive grace.

How is your life a reflection of God's inclusive grace?

_____

Reflection

When things go wrong, we tend to blame something or someone else rather than ourselves. We'll even blame God because of our own expectations in life. We don't see things from a clear and objective perspective.

_____

Prayer Focus

When you find yourself shifting blame to someone other than yourself and not facing your own responsibilities, ask the Lord to show you His perspective of your situation. Ask Him to help you learn a better way to handle things.

SCRIPTURE TEXT
RUTH 4:13-22

*So Boaz took Ruth and she became his wife. When he made love to her, the L*ORD *enabled her to conceive, and she gave birth to a son.*

*The women said to Naomi: "Praise be to the L*ORD*, who this day has not left you without a guardian-redeemer. May he become famous throughout Israel!*

He will renew your life and sustain you in your old age. For your daughter-in-law, who loves you and who is better to you than seven sons, has given him birth."

Then Naomi took the child in her arms and cared for him. The women living there said, "Naomi has a son!" And they named him Obed. He was the father of Jesse, the father of David.

This, then, is the family line of Perez: Perez was the father of Hezron,

Hezron the father of Ram, Ram the father of Amminadab,

Amminadab the father of Nahshon, Nahshon the father of Salmon,

Salmon the father of Boaz, Boaz the father of Obed,

Obed the father of Jesse, and Jesse the father of David.

(Ruth 4:13-22 NIV)

QUESTIONS TO REVIEW AND CONSIDER

1. What takes place as the story concludes, in verse 13-17?
2. How does the story shift back to Naomi? What is said to Naomi?
3. Who speaks to her, and what form does it seem to be given in?
4. What is the significance of what these women say to Naomi and about Obed?
5. How is this related to the genealogy at the end of the book?
6. Why would this be important to Israel and their history, especially at the time this was written?
7. How does the story end for Naomi? How does this compare to the beginning of the story?
8. What simple application can be made from this story as a whole?
9. Are there any more personal applications for your own life?

EPILOGUE

I hope you've been encouraged and blessed by these devotional studies. If you skipped the questions, let me encourage you to take your Bible, a pen and notebook, and some quiet time to go back through the Book of Ruth and review and answer these questions.

Looking at these Stories of Redemption drawn from the book of Ruth, it's important to consider how each one relates to us in a personal way. The significance of Ruth's inclusion into the Messianic birth line is essential for understanding the greatness of God's grace.

God's redemption provides both a reconciliation with God bringing freedom from sin's grip, and a restoration of relationship with God for moving forward by faith.

As said before,

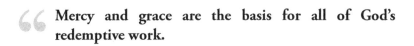 **Mercy and grace are the basis for all of God's redemptive work.**

and…

Restoration is always the intent of the Lord in redemption.

These insights, above all, is what I hope you gain and takeaway from these devotions. I also encourage you to keep these insights uppermost in your mind and deep within your heart. This is the message of God many people have yet to hear or understand.

May the Lord bless and confirm these truths in your life so you're able to share them with others, especially those who've never heard or grasped the greatness of God and His redemption for all humanity.

Only by God's redemptive grace,

ENDNOTES

8. When We Try to Help God

1. https://www.gotquestions.org/four-spiritual-laws.html

ACKNOWLEDGMENTS

I'm thankful for those who've helped me with publishing this book, especially when it came to editing!

Thanks to Ruth O'Neil for her comprehensive editing skills, and to Laura Ali for the fine-tuning of her editing work!

Thanks to Laura Williams for the custom art work and for her husband Daniel setting up the title page graphics for the cover and other graphics!

Thanks for the input and insight of my good friends Bruce and Jeff regarding the narrative of these stories.

I'm also thankful for the many students and listeners who sat through the many times I've taught through the Book of Ruth including the devotionals on my blog that these stories are based on. All of it was preparation for this book.

And, as always, I'm thankful for the Lord opening my eyes, mind, and heart to see and understand what He made known to me in the process of writing these stories!

ABOUT THE AUTHOR

I've had the privilege of planting a church in the US and establishing two ministries overseas, as well as many other ministry experiences.

I have a passion to disciple and mentor leaders and pastors within the US and overseas and love to teach and train leaders whenever possible.

Writing is a major part of what I do for the past several years. My writing projects include a book, training materials, and Bible studies for leaders and cross-cultural missions. I also post articles, devotionals, and Bible studies on my site— Word-Strong.com

I've served as a chaplain in a local restaurant and small business, and am one of several pastors serving with Poimen Ministries.

Made in the USA
Columbia, SC
18 January 2023

75585787R00068